IQRA' Kindergarten Curriculum

Volume 4:
Fiqh and 'Ibadat

Tasneema Ghazi
PhD Curriculum, University of Minnesota

IQRA'
International Educational Foundation
Chicago

**Part of a Comprehensive
and Systematic Program
of Islamic Studies**

Editors and Reviewers:

Noura Durkee
M.A. Fine Arts, Stanford University

Shahida Ali Khan
Principal, New Horizon School, California

Artists and Designers

Saba Ghazi
B.A. Fine Arts, University of Illinois

Usama Ghazi
Student, University of Redlands

Mike Rezac
B.A. Fine Arts, University of llinois

**Under the Auspices of
Educational Program
Development Committee:**

Dr. M.A.W. Fakhri, Chairman

Br. Fadel Abdullah

Br. Mohammad Nur Abdullah

Dr. Abidullah Ghazi, Secretary

Dr. Tasneema Ghazi

Dr. Mohammad Kishta

Dr. Sulayman Nyang

Acknowledgements:

Iqra' Charitable Society
for their support and
establishment of the Chair
of Curriculum Development

Islamic Society of North America and
International Institute of Islamic Thought
for participation in the evaluation
and publication effort.

ISBN # 1-56316-254-7

IQRA's Note

We at IQRA' International Educational Foundation are grateful to Allah (SWT) for enabling us to present the second level, kindergarten, of its integrated Islamic curriculum.

The present volume of IQRA' Curriculum (Kindergarten Fiqh and 'Ibadat), represents four years of painstaking research, study, writing and field testing by Dr. Tasneema Ghazi, IQRA's Director of Curriculum. She was assisted by our able team members of the Program Development Committee, innumerable educators, teachers, community workers, and concerned parents.

IQRA' is pleased to announce that its plans to develop, field test and publish an integrated curriculum for Islamic schools from preschool to high school within the next five years (by July 1997) are well under way.

The development and production of this curriculum is part of IQRA's vision of a comprehensive system of Islamic education which covers:

1. An integrated curriculum from preschool to high school.

2. A comprehensive program of Islamic Studies at all levels to include ten basic Islamic subjects and to cover graded *textbooks*, *workbooks*, *enrichment literature, parents/teachers manual* and *educational aids*.

3. An Open University and Home based education.

In each area Iqra's work is progressing in a planned way and we hope within this decade (before we enter the year 2000) IQRA's vision will become a reality, *InshaAllah*.

This kind of effort needs: i) a commitment to make Islamic education our foremost priority, ii) mobilization of communities' human and financial resources, iii) institutionalization of efforts and iv) coordination with other organizations.

We urge all concerned Muslims and Islamic organizations to cooperate with IQRA' and become an *Ansar* of its Educational Program.

Let us together establish IQRA' International Educational Foundation as the finest institution of Islamic educational research and development; it would be the best gift, we the North American Muslims, can give to our children and to the *Ummah* as a whole.

Dedicated To:

Dr. Abdullah Omar Nassief
Our friend, guide and philosopher
An embodiment of the spirit of early Islam

Who

In response to the basic need of Islamic education
upported IQRA' International Educational Foundation
in the fulfillment of its Educational Vision

KINDERGARTEN PROGRAM
IN
AN ISLAMIC SCHOOL

PHILOSOPHY:

The goal of the Kindergarten Program in an Islamic school is to provide opportunities for an active involvement of children, their parents and teachers in a continual process of education based on the knowledge of the Qur'an and the *Sunnah*. Involvement of Muslim parents in the educational process of their children is specially important due to the many non-Islamic influences of the modern Western culture and environment.

Kindergarten is usually the beginning of formal schooling, even though in many educational systems it is not compulsory for a five years old to attend regular school. When a child enters Kindergarten, both he and his parents begin a far reaching experience. For many children this is the first experience of formal schooling and for many parents this is the first encounter with being separated from their child. Kindergarten teachers and school administrators need to plan on building a relationship of trust and understanding between school and home. Once established, this relationship provides many avenues for coordination and cooperation between these two primary institutions in the life of a child.

The source of every Islamic educational program should be the "Revelation" as opposed to pure "reason", as reason without the light of the Revelation is misguided and limited. The curriculum planners, the administrators, the teachers and the parents of Islamic schools should make continuous efforts to integrate Islamic knowledge , behavior, *Akhlaq* and *Adab* in the daily activities of each classroom . Any objective, content and activity which is in conflict with the clear teachings of the Qur'an and the *Sunnah* has no place in a classroom for Muslim children. Thus, it is important that those who are involved in educating and nurturing our children should have a comprehensive knowledge of the Qur'an and the *Sunnah* and as the models of Islamic behavior and living, practice the teachings in their daily lives.

The goal of the program should be the development of an Islamic personality through inculcation of Islamic values and nurturing of Islamic behavior. Keeping in mind the cognitive, social, motor, emotional and physical characteristics of five and six year olds, the emphasis should be on the development of Islamic concepts and acquisition of Islamic practices. The teachers, administrators and older children should be the role model of Islamic behavior and living for the Kindergartners who learn and adopt new behaviors easily and quickly from those, they idealize. The importance of learning which takes place during the kindergarten years has been best stated by Robert Fulghum in the following words;

1

All I really need to know I learned in Kindergarten

All I really need to know about how to live and what to do and how to be
I learned in Kindergarten. Wisdom was not at the top of the graduate -school
mountain, but there in the sandpile at Sunday School. These are the things I
learned. Share everything. Play fair. Don't hit people. Put things back where
you found them. Clean up your own mess. ....

(Robert Fulghum)

To achieve the goals, the Kindergarten program should provide for the child:

1) Opportunities for physical, social, motor, emotional, cognitive and moral development to the extent of his and her capabilities and the rate of his or her own development.

2) An Islamic environment so that the moral and spiritual I self of the child can develop under the teachings of the Qur'an and the *Sunnah.*

3) A secure and safe environment so that the child will not be afraid to try new experiences.

4) Varied kind of experiences for learning, mastering and completing developmental tasks.

5) Warm and supportive adults to guide and encourage both individual and group activities and to act as suitable Muslim role models for the children.

6) Freedom, opportunities and encouragement towards developing responsibility, self control and independence with respect for others.

7) Loving, clear and meaningful beginning lessons in the teachings of the Qur'an, *Hadith, Sirah,* Islamic *Akhlaq,* Islamic *Fiqh & 'Ibadat* and Islamic history providing a foundation for a lifetime of practice and study.

CHARACTERISTICS OF YOUNG CHILDREN
BETWEEN THE AGES OF FIVE AND SIX YEARS

Children between the ages of five and six years are approaching the end of the period of Early Childhood. Following are some of the specific characteristics of five and six year olds.

PHYSICAL:

"A normally active Kindergartner is a busy, curious and industrious child" (Harris et.al, 1986, p. 323).   He manages his body movements with more skill and comfort. He can walk backward with toe and heel pattern. Can run fast, skip, hop and play games. He is able to balance on one foot, jump and land on toes, jump down two or three steps.

He can take care of himself by washing without splashing water on his clothes, dressing himself and tying his shoe laces.   A Kindergarten child enjoys water play, building with blocks and large boxes , can build three dimensional structures. He can use tools such as scissors, screw drivers and hammer etc, . Working with the puzzles is one of the favorite play for the children between the ages of five and six .

Fine motor coordination develops to a point where he is able to copy triangle and diamond. He can begin to print some letters or numbers and his name correctly. Can draw recognizable life like representations and a definite preference for left or right handedness is established.

VISION:

The five and six year olds can coordinate the senses of touch, hearing and vision almost as well as adults. As opposed to three and four year-olds who rely more on touch while exploring the environment, the five and six year-olds rely more on vision (White et.al, 1964). Thus, while exploring the unfamiliar objects three and four year-olds depend more on the sense of TOUCH, whereas five and six year olds pay more attention to the color and size of the object and use more visual clues.

COGNITIVE:

Children between the ages of five and six years are still at the "pre-operational stage" where symbolic thinking dominates much of their life. Symbolic thinking enables them to have a schema of the words and images represent an object or certain actions in the mind of the child. He is capable of using language more meaningfully.However, this ability of symbolic thinking is accompanied by important characteristics referred by Piaget as "Egocentrism", "Animism" , "Finalism: and "Centration".

Egocentrism is the condition where children think and experience every event in relation to themselves. Even the phenomenon of nature happen because of them as the center, for example the sun rises to make them feel happy and for them to play outside, night falls to make them sleep , Mom and Dad go to work to get money for them to buy things etc.

Animism refers to the child's tendency to attribute life like qualities to inanimate objects for example, attributing pain and happiness to dolls and stuffed animals. However, by the age five and six they begin to move away from this condition and have some idea of the differences between animate and inanimate objects. They still make errors in judgement.

Finalism is the belief of the pre-operational child that every action accomplishes some purposes. The "purposes" attributed to each action is unique to each child. They believe that every movement (by human or an object) is "goal directed" because their own movements are goal directed.

Centration refers to the inclination of the pre-operational child to concentrate only on a single aspect of a situation and neglect all others. They do not understand that a change in the appearance of certain object does not necessarily mean that the object has lost many other of its attributes. For example they believe that a tall slender glass holds more water than a shorter wide glass, even though they both have the capacity of holding the same amount of water.

Concept Formation is one of the most important achievements of early childhood years. "Concepts" according to Piaget, ' are cognitive categories that help children and adults organize information and acquire new knowledge'. Environment provided for the children during these early years helps in the development of specific concept, which makes the role of "important adults" in the life of children significantly important.

LANGUAGE DEVELOPMENT:

Language development takes place at a very fast pace to help the child express his own ideas. The vocabulary grows to 8,000 - 14,000 words by age six. Length of the sentences increases from three words per sentence at age 2-3 to 6-8 words per sentence by the ages five and six years. More "WH' words are used (why, whom, where and when). Children tend to ask more questions.

SOCIAL DEVELOPMENT:

Five and six year-olds develop more social skills which are reflected in their play which becomes more associative and co-operative. They play together to help each other in the achievement of certain goal. There is a tendency to help each other during play and other activities.

Kindergarten children are more ready for a few hours' separation from their parents than the younger children. They are ready to share, be considerate to other, wait for their turn and accept small responsibility (when required to do so) in the classroom. According to Piaget children between the ages of three and five believe that the rules are generated by an external authority such as God, parents or teachers and can not be changed . However, due to egocentrism, they practice their own version of rules, ignoring or changing the existing rules.

EMOTIONAL DEVELOPMENT

The Kindergarten child is still quite egocentric, even though he becomes more considerate of others. Most of the fears of early childhood begin to subside. Five and six year-olds are more willing to accept the reasoning and explanations for the occurrences which frighten them. They tend to pay attention to the causes (given to them) of why and how things happen. In short, they can distinguish between the reality and the fantasy. Anger is expressed more verbally and physically than in the temper tantrums. They are ready to accept and follow the rules.

Teachers and parents should be aware of the feelings and emotions of the children. Adults should be sensitive to the expressed feelings of the children. It is difficult for them at this stage to keep up with their own pace. For example, they strive to do too many things by themselves but when things build up and become too much to handle, the teachers and parents should give a helping hand. The children have to understand that it is okay to be dependent upon someone for a while.

Classroom activities should be planned keeping in mind the above characteristics of the children.

FIQH AND 'IBADAT

PHILOSOPHY

Fiqh means "understanding and knowledge". Thus, *Fiqh* actually is a branch of knowledge which defines and clarifies the Islamic ways of worship and living. Great scholars, the *Fuqaha'* have worked deligently on defining and interpreting the Islamic laws in the light of the Qur'an and the *Sunnah*.

We, at Iqra' believe that the seeds of learning about *Fiqh* should be sown at an early age, as *Fiqh* constitutes the laws regarding the practices of a Muslim at every step of his or her life, chidlren should be taught and trained to understand and practice the five pillars of Islam. They should learn and adopt the right conduct, *Ma'ruf* and refrain from what is wrong, *Munkar.*

During the early grades the emphasis should be placed on the education and training in Islamic ways of living. Islamic beliefs and practices should permeate through every strand of the curriculum. The teachers and the principal should be the model of a *Mu'min,* guiding the younger generations. At the elementary level, the curriculum focuses on the very basic laws and practices of Islam, as agreed by scholars (*fuqaha'*) of all major schools of *Fiqh.* Emphasis, here is on the development of basic concepts of *'Iman* and Islamic practices. Children are helped in developing their identity as Believers (*Mu'minun*). They are trained to incorporate Islamic ettiquettes and manners in their daily activities.

We believe that the foundation of Islamic ettiquetes and manners should be laid at an early age, thus concepts and practices of Islamic ettiquettes and manners are an integral part of the *Fiqh & 'Ibadat* curriculum at each grade level.

Special attention is paid to helping children develop a habit of using the Islamic vocabulary in their daily use of language at home and in the school. This helps them to remember Allah (SWT) many times during the day. It also helps them to identify themselvels with the other members of the *Ummah* speaking the same language and practising the same morals.

The goals of Islamic education and training program of Iqra' International Eduational Foundation is to help young children to grow up to be those ideal members of the community, who in the words of Allah (SWT);

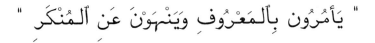

"Invite to what is good and prohibit from what is bad"

HOW TO USE THE CURRICULUM GUIDE

We have made an attempt to develop a comprehensive and integrated curriculum guide, covering five areas of Islamic education viz:

> Teachings of the Qur'an
> *Sirah* of Prophet Muhammad (S)
> *Fiqh* and *Ibadat*
> Islamic History
> Islamic *Akhlaq* and *Adab*

The curriculum guide is integrated in the sense that there are constant cross references of goals, objectives and suggested activities from one subject area to the other. A teacher teaching all five subjects to the same grade or level can take advantage of this scheme of integration. However, keeping in mind the needs of the teachers who teach only one subject, the curriculum for each subject at each level is kept quite independent. Following are some special features of this curriculum guide:

Statement of the Philosophy

The Curriculum guide opens with a philosophy statement. We request everyone of you to read the statement and develop a solid and clearly defined philosophical basis for your school and your classroom.

Characteristics of children between the ages of five and six years

Under this heading is a brief description of the physical, cognitive, social and emotional development of Kindergarten age children. We urge you to read it and try to understand the behavior and learning process of children under your supervision while in school. Most of the teachers and parents will need more information about the developmental process of young children than provided here , which can be easily obtained by reading any of the recommended books on Child Development.(See Bibliography).

Scope and Sequencece chart

This chart represents the total sequence of the units to be covered during the course of one academic year of Kindergarten. SCOPE refers to the amount of information which is made available to the children at a particular grade level.

For example the Sequence of "Islamic History " component of the Kindergarten curriculum is from Adam (A) to Prophet Ibrahim (A) . The history of the prophets is introduced in the same chronological order as mentioned in the Qur'an, thus, following five prophets are introduced in the sequence:

Adam (A)---- Nuh (A)----Hud (A) ----- Salih (A) -------and Ibrahim (A)
The next eight will be introduced in the First grade and the rest in the third and fourth grades, *InshaAllah.* The Scope of Islamic history curriculum is determined keeping in mind the physical, cognitive, social and emotional development of children between the ages of five to eight years. Amount of time available to the teacher of Islamic history is also an important contributing factor in determining the Scope.

THE SCHEME

Unit: Total spectrum of selected topics is divided into Units. A Unit represents a topic or an area of study. Each Unit is divided into many Lessons. Each Lesson is developed around one aspect of the Unit. Some units are larger and have more Lessons than others.

Each Unit begins with specific "Learning Experiences and Activities" to be developed through various lessons. Please read them carefully so you are aware of them during your lesson planning and teaching. Following the rules of curriculum integration, "learning experiences" in various areas of learning are imbedded within each Unit.It is suggested that special attention should be paid to these details.

Lesson: Each Lesson consists of:

Focal Point is the theme of the lesson---the goal itself.

Behavioral objectives are the objectives of the lesson stated in measurable behavioral terms. It is hoped that children , after successfully completing the lesson, will be able to demonstrate the desired changes in their daily behavior. Teachers and parents should make sure that the intended behavior is learned and acquired by each child after the completion of each lesson. Mastery of these behavioral Objectives by each child is essential for continuous learning and concept formation.

Suggested Activities are only "suggested" activities to help the teachers plan their lesson. By no means any teacher is bound to use only these activities. We encourage you to be innovative, plan your own activities, use those suggested or even improvise the suggested activities according to your need. No matter what you as the teacher do just remember that you have to have well developed lesson plans before entering the classroom. It is also important to plan some time during the class period for children's participation and interaction . Sometimes the worksheets are provided for the teachers to use in the class.

Evaluation Forms At the end of each Unit, there is an evaluation form, that is for us. We would like you to take some time and complete the form after completing each Unit and mail it to our offices. This is our way of involving you in the process of curriculum development and field testing. Your input as the person in the classroom using the curriculum guide is absolutely essential for the validity of this curriculum. This is the first draft for field testing and evaluation.

Please feel free to get in touch with us at the Iqra' Foundation. We welcome your valuable comments and suggestions

A NOTE TO THE TEACHERS:

It is important to remember that the two very common modern ideas; **progress** and **evolution** are the running theme of almost all science and educational literature. Most of the films children will see, and many books they will read assume biological and social evolution. Remember to point to the children that the first conscious human being Adam (A) knew more than anyone knows today about the truth and reality. Also remind them that the best moral society that ever will be -- existed in Madinah 1400 years ago during the time of Muhammad Rasulullah (S) and the *Khulafa' Ar-Rashidun.* Point out that the best among us are those who obey Allah (SWT) and follow the Qur'an and the *Sunnah* in their daily living .

As Muslims, we must follow the example of the Madinah society in both our personal and community lives. The truth of *Tawhid* and the reality of leading a moral and virtuous life has been a constant theme in human history, explained to us through the examples of the prophets and the teachings of the revelations. Human society has progressed materially, however, it needs a moral foundation to hold itself together. Each human society must understand and implement these messages and the teachings in their social life, so that it is not completely lost in the material pursuits.

Unit 1: Identity of Self as a Muslim

lessons 1-3

UNIT ONE
LEARNING EXPEREINCES AND ACTIVITIES

1. ## Learning Concepts (Moral Perspectives)

   Identity of self as a Muslim
   Islamic greetings
   Islamic names
   Islamic dress code
   Use of Islamic vocabulary
   Similarities and differences between Muslims and members of other religious groups

2. ## Learning Skills

   Vocabulary
   Comparison - Similarities and differences
   Islamic greetings

3. ## Islamic Habits and Practices

   Using Islamic greetings
   Saying *Bismillah* when beginning to do something
   Following Islamic dress code
   Learning to use Islamic voabulary

4. ## Linguistic Perspective

   Linstening
   Oral language
   Sight vocabulary

5. ## Artistic Expressions

   Songs
   Finger Plays
   Coloring and pasting

TIME REQUIREMENTS

Time Needed: 3-4 class period (45 minutes each)
              + 1 class period for evaluation

IQRA' KINDERGARTEN CURRICULUM
FIQH AND IBADAT

Unit 1: Identity of Self as a Muslim

Lesson 1: Islamic Greetings

FOCAL POINT	PERFORMANCE OBJECTIVES	SUGGESTED ACTIVITIES	RESOURCE MATERIAL
A> When Muslims meet each other, they greet with *Assalamu Alaikum*.	**The children will:** -greet their family members and visitors at home with *"Assalamu Alaikum wa Rahmatullahi wa Barakatahu"*. **Vocabulary:** *Assalamu-Alaikum, wa Alaikum Assalam.*	**The Teacher will:** a. Greet the parents with *Assalamu Alaikum wa Rahmatullahi wa Barakatahu* when they drop their children off at school. b. Send a note home explaining the importance of Islamic greetings and emphasizing that they should be observed at home. c. Tell the children when they need to say Islamic greetings. d. When a child is asked to present a progam in the morning assembly, they should always start with *"Assalamu Alaikum"*. e. Children color picture of people greeting each other with *"Assalamu Alaikum"*. f. Sing *"We are Muslims, Our Deen is Islam. Assalamu Alaikum wa Alaikum Asalaam and When I see a Muslim I say Salam-Asalaamu Alaikum wa Alaikum Assalam"* (See <u>A</u>). g. Have the children do the coloring sheet (See <u>B</u>).	Coloring sheets Crayons, Colored markers, Worksheet

When I Meet a Muslim

We are all Muslims
Our Deen Al-Islam
Assalamu Alaikum
Wa Alaikum Assalam

When I meet a Muslim
I say salam
Assalamu Alaikum
Wa Alaikum Assalam

When I greet somone I say:

الَسَّلَامُ عَلَيْكُمْ

ASSALĀMU ʿALAIKUM

(PEACE BE WITH YOU)

IQRA' KINDERGARTEN CURRICULUM
FIQH AND IBADAT
Unit 1: Identity of Self as a Muslim
Lesson 1: Islamic Greetings
Worksheet B

18

IQRA' KINDERGARTEN CURRICULUM

FIQH and IBADAT

UNIT 1: Identity of self as a "Muslim"

Lesson 2 : Starting every task with "*Bismillah -ir-Rahman-ir-Rahim*" (In the name of Allah, the Compassionate, the Merciful)

FOCAL POINT	PERFORMANCE OBJECTIVES	SUGGESTED ACTIVITIES	RESOURCE MATERIAL
A> It is important for us to begin any work with the name of Allah (SWT) and to ask for His help.	**The Children will:** -Say *Bismillah-ir-Rahman-ir-Rahim* before starting to do anything. -Children will understand the meaning of these words. **Vocabulary:** Merciful Compassionate	**The Teacher will:** a. Read a story to the children and say *Bismillah-ir-Rahman ir-Rahim*, loudly and slowly at the beginning and ask the children to repeat it after her. b. Take the children to wash their hands and have them say *Bismillah-ir- Rahman-ir-Rahim* when they start. c. Ask the children to say it aloud whenever they are starting a project so it becomes habit for them. d. Check at various times throughout the year to see if the children recite *Bismillah-ir-Rahman-ir-Rahim* as a habit. e. At snack or lunch time say *Bismillah-ir-Rahman-ir-Rahim* (when the children start to eat) aloud as a group. f. If all the children have not developed the habit of saying *Bismillah-ir-Rahman-ir-Rahim*, make time to allow for those children to develop this habit. g. Have the children do the worksheet (See <u>A</u>).	Crayons Colored pens Worksheets

IQRA' KINDERGARTEN CURRICULUM
FIQH AND IBADAT
UNIT 1: Identity of Self as a Muslim
Lesson 2: Starting every task with "*Bismillah-ir-Rahman-ir-Rahim*"
Worksheet A

20

IQRA' KINDERGARTEN CURRICULUM
FIQH and IBADAT
UNIT 1: IDENTITY OF SELF AS A "MUSLIM"
Lesson 3: *IMAN:* necessary for Muslims

FOCAL POINT	PERFORMANCE OBJECTIVES	SUGGESTED ACTIVITIES	RESOURCE MATERIAL
A> A Muslim must have Iman	**The children will:** -Believe and say that Allah (SWT) is the only God and Creator of everything and everyone. -Believe and say that Muhammad Rasullulah (S) is His Messenger and Prophet.	**The Teacher will:** **a.** Teach the children the recitation of *Shahadah* in Arabic and its meaning in English. **b.** Write *Shahadah* on a poster board with the English meaning and hang it in the classroom. **c.** Make a cardboard puzzle of *Shahadah* in Arabic. (See "A" below) **d.** Help the children memorize the *Shahadah* by repeating it during various activities. **e.** Evaluation -Ask each child to be a leader for an activity and recite the *Shahada* before starting each activity with the rest of the children reciting it aloud at the same time.	Posterboard IQRA' chart of Shahadah Cardboard

our Kalimah is:

LA ILAHA ILLALLAHU
MUHAMMADUN RASUL ULLAH

(THERE IS NO GOD BUT ALLAH, MUHAMMAD IS THE MESSENGER OF ALLAH)

I am a Muslim and Allah Made Me

I am a Muslim and Allah made me.
   Allah made my eyes
   So I can see the Sun rise!
I am a Muslim and Allah made me.
   Allah made my nose,
   So I can smell a rose!
I am a Muslim and Allah made me.
   Allah made my teeth,
   So that I can eat!
I am a Muslim and Allah made me.
   Allah made my ear
   So that I can hear!
I am a Muslim and Allah made me.
   Allah made my knee
   How fast I can flee!
I am a Muslim and Allah made me.
   Allah made my feet,
   See me walk across the street!
I am a Muslim and Allah made me.
   Allah made my toes
   and placed them in neat rows.
I am a Muslim and Allah made me.
   (etc. with other body parts)

Ending:

   Allah made my eyes, nose, teeth,
   ear, knee, feet, toes ...
   (Point to each part as you sing the end)

IQRA' Kindergarten Curriculum

Unit 2: Iman (Tawhid)

lessons 1-3

UNIT TWO

LEARNING EXPERIENCES AND ACTIVITIES

1. Learning Concepts (Moral Perspective)

Belief in Allah (SWT) as the only Creator
Belief in Allah's power
Belief in Alah's merc and compassion
Beleif that Allah is all-knowing
Readiness to follow Allah's commands
Concept of Obedience
Reliance on Allah (SWT)
Patience
Obedience
Prayers

2. Learning Skills and Habits

Asking for Allah's forgiveness
Asking for Allah's Mercy
Asking for Allah's help
Learnig to be patience
Learning to obedient
Critical thinking skills
Vocabulary

3. Linguistic Perspective

Listening
Oral language
Vocabulary
Sight Vocabulary

TIME REQUIREMENTS

Time Needed   4 class hours +One class hour for Evaluation

IQRA' KINDERGARTEN CURRICULUM
FIQH AND IBADAT
UNIT 2: *IMAN (TAWHID)*
Lesson 1: Allah (SWT) is the only Creator

FOCAL POINT	PERFORMANCE OBJECTIVES	SUGGESTED ACTIVITIES	RESOURCE MATERIAL
A> Allah (SWT) has created everyone and everything.	**The Children will:** -believe that everyone of is created by Allah (SWT). **Skills:** Reading and decoding Matching and labeling Cutting and pasting	**The Teacher will:** a. Collect family pictures of the children. b. In a group situation while all children are sitting close together on a rug, show pictures of the family of each child. Encourage the children to take turns talking about their family members. c. Ask children that who has created our fathers, mothers, brothers and sisters? d. Remind the children that we should always thank Allah (SWT) for His blessings. e. Do the family exercises with the children (See A, B & C). f. Ask the children to cut and paste the picutres of some of the things that Allah has created on a large sheet of poster board. g. Seat the children on the floor and ask them questions about Allah's creations, eg: -How do trees grow? -What do they need to grow? (water & soil) -Who makes the seeds grow? -Where so they get the water? (rain) -Who sends the water and food? (Allah SWT) -Why do you think Allah (SWT) takes care of trees?	Family photographs of the children in the class. Paste, Paper, Scissors, Pictures of families of animals, reptiles, insects & birds etc.

Allah (SWT) made Families

28

Every Family is Created by Allah (SWT)

Objectives

1. Practice in grouping, sorting and categorizing.

2. Show that families belong together because that is how Allah (SWT) has created them.

Materials Needed

-Pictures from **Worksheet A** of assorted animal families
-Scissors, glue, paper and crayons

Procedures

1. Show the students the animals from the previous worksheet (A).

2. Explain that the members of each animal family look similar but not exactly alike.

3. Explain the different types of families (nuclear. extended etc.) and different family members.

4. Have the children color the animals on the sheets (if they haven,t already one Worksheet A)

5. Instruct the children to cut and paste the animals on a separate sheet of paper, grouping members of each family of together.

6. The children may label the members of the family. (Father, Mother, Baby etc).

IQRA' KINDERGARTEN CURRICULUM
FIQH & IBADAT
UNIT 2: IMAN (TAWHID)
Lesson 1: Allah (SWT) is the Only Creator
Worksheet C (This lesson can be integrated with the lesson on Science and growing things, especially seeds and plants.)

Allah (SWT) Created Plants

-Plan a planting activity with children (see Science Curr. Unit 1)
-Set apart a table for this activity. Work in small groups of 4-6 children at a time.

Materials needed:

Crayons, potting soil, glue, small pots, paper, water, paint, tongue depressors, seeds, plant bulbs and construction paper

Procedure

(Begin with *Bismillah -ir-Rahman -ir-Rahim).*

1. Cut the construction paper into square and circular pieces, and write the names of the students on them (one name per piece). Glue each name tag on a tongue depressor.

2. Give a small pot to each child.

3. Let them put the potting soil in the planter until it is half full.

4. Ask them to pick the desired seeds (there should be a variety of seeds that are properly marked and labeled in containers on a table).

5. Show them how to cover the seeds with more potting soil.

6. Help them to say *Bismillah-ir-Rahman-ir-Rahim* as they put a little water in the pot.

7. Each child should place their tongue depressors, marked with his/her name into the pot.

8. Each child should place their pot in a predesignated area.

Follow Up

-Remind the children to water their plants and observe their growth.
-Keep one of the plants out of light and refrain from watering another. Allow the children to observe the effects.

Discussion

-When almost all of the plants have sprouted, discuss in a group how Allah (SWT) has helped the plants to grow.
-Discuss (generally) how water, heat, soil and the sun are all necessary for plants to grow.
-Discuss how experimental plants were less successful, because we were trying to raise them against the nature.
-Explain that people also need fresh and clean air, light and water given to us by Allah.
-Explain that we must always remember Allah, because he makes us grow too.

IQRA' KINDERGARTEN CURRICULUM
FIQH and IBADAT
UNIT 2: *IMAN (TAWHID)*
Lesson 2: No One Shares Allah's Power

FOCAL POINT	PERFORMANCE OBJECTIVES	SUGGESTED ACTIVITIES	RESOURCE MATERIAL
A> No one shares Allah's powers.	**The Children will:** -reject any notion of duality and have faith in *Tawhid Insha Allah.* -understand that Allah is the only God and therefore the only One with such powers.	**The Teacher will:** a. Introduce the lesson with the recitation of *the Shahada* in Arabic in unison. b. Discuss the meaning in English c. Play the "Follow the Leader" game. (See <u>A</u>) d. Discuss with the children what it means to be only "One". e. Talk about the second part of *Shahadah;* that Muhammad (S) is the *Rasul* of Allah. f. Tell the children the meaning of <u>*Rasul,*</u> in an introductory fashion.	

Follow the Leader Game

As the teacher you will be the leader. Ask the children to pay attention and follow the orders you give in this exercise eg. "Put your hands on your head", "Touch your feet",etc.

Get another adult to act as a second leader, explain to the children that they must now follow <u>two</u> leaders instead of just <u>one.</u>

Both leaders (you and the other adult) Start to give different commands at the same time. For example:

<u>Teacher</u>: "Put your hand on your head"
<u>2nd Adult</u>: "Put your hands on your stomach"

<u>Teacher</u>: "Touch your right ear"
<u>2nd Adult</u>: "Touch your nose"

Soon, the children will be confused about the double commands. At this point, stop and discuss why and how it was impossible to follow two different leaders. Then conclude that there can be only one leader giving commands, or their is disorder. Relate this point to the fact that there can be only one Allah (SWT).

IQRA' KINDERGARTEN CURRICULUM
FIQH and IBADAT
UNIT 2: *IMAN (TAWHID)*
Lesson 3: Allah (SWT) is Compassionate and Merciful

FOCAL POINT	PERFORMANCE OBJECTIVES	SUGGESTED ACTIVITIES	RESOURCE MATERIAL
A> Allah (SWT) is Merciful and Compassionate	The Children will: -understand that Allah (SWT) has instilled a love for children in the hearts parents. -understand that Allah (SWT) is forgiving. -learn to ask for Allah's forgiveness. -learn to ask for Allah's mercy when in difficulty and at all times.	The Teacher will: a. Introduce the lesson with some guiding activity. b. Show the children a book of animal mothers and fathers taking care of their babies and children. c. Talk about how parents love their babies and do everything for them. Explain that it is Allah (SWT) who has placed this love for children in hearts of parents. e. Allah (SWT) loves all of us just like parents love their children. He loves us even more. f. Tell the children some stories in which Allah (SWT) forgave people or a person who committed a sin (eg. Adam (A)). g. Write language experience stories told by the children from their experiences when they asked for Allah's help and mercy.	Books of animals, babies, their mothers and fathers. (see bibliography) Large writing pad, Marker

IQRA' KINDERGARTEN CURRICULUM
FIQH AND IBADAT
UNIT 2: *IMAN (TAWHID)*
Lesson 4: Following Allah's Commands

FOCAL POINT	PERFORMANCE OBJECTIVES	SUGGESTED ACTIVITIES	RESOURCE MATERIA
A> Inculcation of obedience to Allah (SWT)	The Children will: -be obedient and follow Allah's commands. -Obey their teachers, parents and other adults.	The Teacher will: a. Greet the children with "*Assalam-u-Alaikum*". b. Talk about the meaning of obedience at the children's level. c. Discuss different ways in which we can thank Allah (SWT). d. Ask the children to describe incidents in which they followed one of Allah's commands. e. Talk about some of the teachings of Allah (SWT) in the Qur'an. f. Do the song activity with the children (See A)	

34

ALLAH'S GIFT

Allah gave us five counting fingers *(Show the five fingers)*

Thumb is one, have some fun

Pointer two, I see you

Tallman three, like a tree

Ringman four, now one more

Weeman five, swim and dive

Throughout the song the teacher should use his or her fingers and encourage the children to do the same while singing the song. After singing the song a few times discuss with the children many gifts of Allah (SWT).

Ask the children several questions. For eg:
-*Who has given us hands,fingers,eyes and nose etc.?*
-*What else Allah (SWT) has given us?*
-*What should we say to Allah (SWT) for giving us so much?* *(Thankyou Allah)*

The teacher can talk about how we should listen to Allah's commands and follow the teachings of His Prophet Muhammad (S).

جبرائيل

عزرائيل

اسرافيل

ميكائيل

Unit 3: Belief in the Angels of Allah

lessons 1-2

UNIT THREE

LEARNING EXPERIENCES AND ACTIVITIES

1. Learning Concepts (Moral Perspective)

Belief in the angels of Allah (SWT)
Belief in the purity of the angels
Learning that angels are obedient servants of Allah (SWT)
Learning that angels have limited knowledge as opposed to human beings
Belief in *Wahi*

2. Learning Skills

Vocabulary
Comparison and contrast
Drawing conclusion
Prediction
Recall and recognition

3. Historical Perspective

Story of the creation of Adam (A)
Description of *Wahi* to Prophet Muhammad (S)
Names of four *Muqqrrabun* angels

4. Artistic Perspective

Coloring
Painting
Drawing

TIME REQUIREMENTS

Time Needed: 3 class periods (45 minutes each)
+ 1 period for evaluation

IQRA' KINDERGARTEN CURRICULUM
FIQH AND IBADAT
UNIT 3: BELIEF IN THE ANGELS OF ALLAH (SWT)
Lesson 1: Angels are Special Creations of Allah (SWT)

FOCAL POINT	PERFORMANCE OBJECTIVES	SUGGESTED ACTIVITIES	RESOURCE MATERIAL
A> Angels are one of the creations of Allah (SWT).	The Children will: -learn that angels are created by Allah (SWT).	The Teacher will: a. Ask the children the names of different things that Allah has created, and record their responses. Then tell them that Allah has also created the angels.	Markers, Large Writing Pad
B> Attributes of the angels	-know that angels are made of *Nur*. -learn that angels can see us but we cannot see them. -know that angels are pure and cannot commit sin. -know that Angels always listen to Allah's commands. -understand that angels know only what Allah wants them to know.	a. Tell the children that angels are made of light. b Tell the children that we cannot see the angels, but this does not mean that they don't exist. c. Do the "Close Your Eyes" activity with the children. Have the children close their eyes and tell of what they see or sense around them, so they develop an understanding of the existence of things that are unknown and unseen. d. Tell the children that angels are pure and can do no evil, because they never do what Allah (SWT) doesn't want them to do. e. Tell the children that whenever Allah wants the angels to do something, they do it right away. f. Tell the children about the limited knowledge that the angels have; relate the story of the creation of Adam (A) from the lesson in Islamic History.	The Story of the Creation of Prophet Adam (A)

IQRA' KINDERGARTEN CURRICULUM
FIQH AND IBADAT
UNIT 3: BELIEF IN THE ANGELS OF ALLAH (SWT)
Lesson 2: The Existence of Angels, as Mentioned in the Qur'an and the Hadith

FOCAL POINT	PERFORMANCE OBJECTIVES	SUGGESTED ACTIVITIES	RESOURCE MATERIAL
C> Sources that prove the existence of angels	-believe that angels do exist, as they are mentioned in the Qur'an. -believe that Prophet Muhammad (S), who always told the truth, told us about the angels, and asked that we believe in them. -believe that Angel Jibril visited Muhammad (S) in the Cave of Hira.	**a.** Begin this lesson by asking the children, "How do we know that Allah (SWT) really created any angels, like He created us?". Allow the children to respond, and then inform that Allah has told us about the angels in the Qur'an, and every word in the Qur'an is true. **b.** Recite some of the Ayahs in the Qur'an that mention the existence of angels. **c.** Relate this to the lesson on *Wahi* in Sirah. Inform the children that Muhammad (S) was visited by an angel many times while he was in the Cave of Hira. Ask the children if they know the name of this angel. **d.** Talk about some of the basic differences between us and the angels. Write language experience stories as told by the children.	Large writing pad, Markers
D> **SKILLS** Compare and Contrast	**VOCABULARY** *Nur* *Wahi*		

40

IQRA' KINDERGARTEN CURRICULUM
FIQH AND IBADAT
UNIT 3: BELIEF IN THE ANGELS OF ALLAH (SWT)
Lesson 3: The Names of Some Special Angels

FOCAL POINT	PERFORMANCE OBJECTIVES	SUGGESTED ACTIVITIES	RESOURCE MATERIAL
A> There are many angels	**The Children will:** -know that Allah (SWT) has created many angels, just as He has created many human beings.	**The Teacher will:** **a.** Show the children a globe, and ask them, "Who lives here? Who has Allah created the Earth for? How many people do you think live on the Earth?" Then tell the children that Allah has also created many angels, who live in Heaven, which is another world.	A Globe, or Picture of the Earth
B> The four special angels	-learn the names of the four special angels. -learn the tasks of each of the special angels.	**a.** Tell the children the names of the special angels that Allah (SWT) created. **b.** Write the names of the four special angels on poster board in Arabic, English and English transliteration, so the children know how to spell and pronounce the names. **c.** Teach the children the duties of each of the four special angels.	Poster board, Markers, Crayons
C> Revision and Evaluation of the Unit	-be encouraged to discuss and answer questions about topics they have learned in this unit.	**a.** Make a mobile of the names of the four special angels of Allah. with the names in English on one side, and in Arabic on the other. **b.** Show the children the first few letters of the names of each of the special angels, and have them give the respective names.	Cards, with first few letters of the names on them.

IQRA' Kindergarten Curriculum

Unit 4: Belief in the Scriptures

lessons 1-3

UNIT FOUR
LEARNING EXPERIENCES AND ACTIVITIES

1. Learning Concepts (Moral Perspective)

Belief in the scriptures as the words of Allah (SWT)
Belief that Allah (SWT) has sent His guidance to His prophets.
Learning the names of the prophets who have received the scriptures.
Belief that Qur'an is the last and the final scripture of Allah (SWT)
Understanding the meaning of the "last"
Understanding the difference between a scripture and an ordinary book.
Learning and following some of the teachings of Allah's Scripture.

2. Learning Skills

Vocabulary
Critical thinking skills

3. Historical Perspective

The first and the last Prophets
History of the people of some of the Prophets
Revelation of the Qur'an

TIME REQUIREMENTS

Time Needed: 3 class hours (45 minutes each)

IQRA' KINDERGARTEN CURRICULUM
FIQH AND IBADAT
UNIT 4: BELIEF IN THE SCRIPTURES
Lesson 1: We Believe in the Scriptures Sent by Allah (SWT)

FOCAL POINT	PERFORMANCE OBJECTIVES	SUGGESTED ACTIVITIES	RESOURCE MATERIAL
A> Concept of the Scriptures of Allah (SWT).	The Children will: -learn that Allah (SWT) has sent books to guide us.	The Teacher will: a. Show and share a copy of the Qur'an with the children. b. Share a copy of the Bible and the Towrat and some other books with the children.	Copies of the Qur'an Copies of the Bible & Old Testament
B> The differences between the books of Allah, and books written by human being	-learn that the books of Allah are different from any other book. -learn the ways in which these books differ from books written by human beings.	a. Tell the children that the Qur'an, the Bible and the Towrat are called the Scriptures because they are direct revelations of Allah's words. However, over time people changed parts of the Bible and the Towrat - but Allah has promised to protect the Qur'an from any changes. b. Tell the children that Allah (SWT) sent these books to very special people called Messengers or *Rusuls*. Ask the children why Allah has sent these books to us, and allow them to express their ideas and opinions.	

IQRA' KINDERGARTEN CURRICULUM
FIQH AND IBADAT
UNIT 4: BELIEF IN THE SCRIPTURES
Lesson 2: The Qur'an is the Last Book Sent By Allah (SWT)

FOCAL POINT	PERFORMANCE OBJECTIVES	SUGGESTED ACTIVITIES	RESOURCE MATERIAL
	The Children will:	**The Teacher will:**	
A> The purpose of the Books of Allah (SWT)	-develop a concept of the purpose of Allah (SWT) sending us books.	a. Tell the children the names of the Books of Allah (SWT), and then tell them the Messengers of Allah who received each book. Have them do the worksheet (See A).	Worksheet, Crayons
B> The names of the prophets who brought each of the books	-learn the names of the Books of Allah, and the prophet that each book was sent to.	a. Show the children the activity "Teachings of the Books of Allah" (See B). Ask the children to describe what they see in the chart. Tell the children that these are some of the teachings of the Books of Allah (SWT).	Worksheet, Crayons
C> The Qur'an; the last book of Allah	-know and believe that the Qur'an is the last book of Allah (SWT).	a. Discuss with the children the concepts of first and last. Tell the children that the Qur'an is the last book given to us by Allah (SWT) and there will be no book after it.	
D> The validity and authenticity of the Qur'an	-learn that Allah (SWT) has promised to protect the Qur'an from people who want to change it, so it is still in its original form.	a. Involve the children in some activities, to help them understand the concept of first and last. For example: -The first person in line is _____. -The last person in line is _____. -The first person to come to class was _____. -The last person to come to class was _____. -The first person to finish an activity was _____. -The last person to finish an activity was _____, etc	

SOME OF THE PROPHETS OF ALLAH (SWT) AND THEIR BOOKS

Draw a line connecting each book to the prophet whom it was revealed to.

MUSA (A)

DAWOOD (A)

MUHAMMAD (S)

47

ISA (A)

THE TEACHINGS OF THE BOOKS OF ALLAH (SWT)

Color the following Teachings of the Scriptures

SHARE EQUALLY

48

BE HONEST IN OUR DEALINGS

HELP THE POOR AND THE NEEDY

PRACTICE JUSTICE

RESPECT AND SERVE THE PARENTS

GAIN KNOWLEDGE

IQRA' KINDERGARTEN CURRICULUM
FIQH AND IBADAT
UNIT 4: BELIEF IN THE SCRIPTURES OF ALLAH (SWT)
Lesson 3: The Qur'an was Revealed to Prophet Muhammad (S) through Angel Jibril

FOCAL POINT	PERFORMANCE OBJECTIVES	SUGGESTED ACTIVITIES	RESOURCE MATERIAL
A> The Qur'an the last book, was revealed to Muhammad (S), the last prophet.	**The Children will:** -learn and believe that Allah sent the Qur'an to Prophet Muhammad (S) through the Angel Jibril.	**The Teacher will:** a. Refer to the Chart of "Revealed Books of Allah", showing the children that Muhammad (S) is the last Prophet of Allah (SWT). b. Show the children a picture of the Cave of Hira, and tell them that this is where Angel Jibril first came to the Prophet (S) and revealed the Qur'an to him. c. Discuss with the children the process of revelation (at their level), where the Angel Jibril would recite verses of the Qur'an and the Prophet (S) would repeat after him, and then remember it all.	Chart of "Revealed Books of Allah"

Unit 5: Belief in the Prophet of Allah

lessons 1-3

UNIT FIVE

LEARNING EXPERIENCES AND ACTIVITIES

1. Learning Concepts (Moral Perspective)

Belief in the Messengers of Allah (SWT)
Meaning and concept of a "Messenger"
Understanding that the Prophets of Allah were humans like us, but very special
Some special qualities of the prophets of Allah (SWT)
Understanding that the prophets were role models for us to follow
Obeying Allah (SWT)
Learning to ask for Allah's forgiveness

2. Learning Skills

Vocabulary
Names of the prophets
Critical thinking skills

3. Historical Perspective

Life and times of some of the prophets of Allah (SWT)
Time line --- a sense of the chronology of history
Lessons from the stories of the people of the prophets (As)

4. Artistic Perspective

Songs and fingerplays
Coloring, cutting and pasting

TIME REQUIREMENTS

Time Needed: Three class hours of 45 minutes each.

IQRA' KINDERGARTEN CURRICULUM
FIQH AND IBADAT
UNIT 5: BELIEF IN THE PROPHETS OF ALLAH (SWT)
Lesson 1: Allah (SWT) Sent Messengers to Teach the Human Beings

FOCAL POINT	PERFORMANCE OBJECTIVES	SUGGESTED ACTIVITIES	
A> Belief that the *Rusul* were special people sent by Allah (SWT) to teach us	The Children will: -learn that messengers are used to convey messages from one place or source to another.	The Teacher will: a. Show the children copies of the Qur'an, Ingil and Towrat, and ask them the names of each book. Ask the children why these books are so special.	Copies of the Books of Allah (SWT)
B> We should follow the teachings of the *Rusul*	-learn that Allah sent *the Rusul* with books to teach the people the right path. -learn that it is our duty to follow the teachings of Prophet Muhammad (S), as he was Allah's last messenger	a. Tell the children the names of some of the other prophets who received books from Allah (SWT), like Isa (A), Musa (A), Dawud (A). Tell the children that there were many other prophets that brought Allah's message to the people, and as Muslims we believe in all of these prophets. b. Try to coordinate this lesson with lessons from Islamic History and the stories of the Prophets of Allah (SWT). If the children have already studied these lessons, have them take turns telling different stories. Write language experience stories, as the children take turns dictating. c. Have the children draw and color pictures of their stories, (making sure they do not actually draw pictures of the prophets), and then make books for the children to read from the dictated stories and colored pictures.	Paper, Crayons, Markers, Staplers, Laminating Plastic, etc.

IQRA' KINDERGARTEN CURRICULUM
FIQH AND IBADAT
UNIT 5: BELIEF IN THE PROPHETS OF ALLAH (SWT)
Lesson 2: Adam (A); The First Man and Prophet of Allah (SWT)

FOCAL POINT	PERFORMANCE OBJECTIVES	SUGGESTED ACTIVITIES	RESOURCE MATERIAL
A> Prophets of Allah (SWT) were all human beings, like us	**The Children will:** -know that the prophets of Allah were not supernatural beings, but just like us, only special. -know that the prophets were best human beings created by Allah (SWT) because they always obeyed Him.	**The Teacher will:** **a.** Tell the children the names of some of the Prophets of Allah (SWT), and a *few* facts on the history of each. Have the children color the worksheet of the Prophets of Allah (SWT). (See <u>A</u>) **b.** Tell the children that when we hear the name of a prophet, we should *"Alai-his-Salam"*. Discuss the meaning of this phrase with the children, and help them memorize it.	Worksheet, Crayons
B> Prophet Adam (A) was the first man and prophet created by Allah (SWT)	-know that Adam (A) was the first man and Prophet.	**a.** After explaining that Adam (A) was the first man and prophet, retell the story of his life, or have the children retell it. **b.** After the children finish coloring the pictures in <u>A</u>, have them cut out the pictures, and paste each to a small piece of construction paper, to make flash cards.	Worksheet, Scissors, Paste etc.

56

IQRA' KINDERGARTEN CURRICULUM
FIQH AND IBADAT
UNIT 5 :BELIEF IN THE PROPHETS OF ALLAH (SWT)
Lesson 2: Adam (A); The First Man and Prophet of Allah (SWT)
Worksheet A

PROPHETS OF ALLAH (SWT) COLORING ACTIVITY

ADAM (A)
Creation of the Earth

NUH (A)
The ark and flood

SALIH (A)
The Camel

57

IQRA' KINDERGARTEN CURRICULUM
FIQH AND IBADAT
UNIT 5 : BELIEF IN THE PROPHETS OF ALLAH (SWT)
Lesson 2: Adam (A); The First Man and Prophet of Allah (SWT)
Worksheet A

MUHAMMAD (S)
The Qur'an

IBRAHIM (A)
Building the Kabah

HUD (A)
The Buildings and People of Aad

IQRA' KINDERGARTEN CURRICULUM
FIQH AND IBADAT
UNIT 5: BELIEF IN THE PROPHETS OF ALLAH (SWT)
Lesson 3: Prophet Muhammad (S); The Last Prophet Of Allah (SWT)

FOCAL POINT	PERFORMANCE OBJECTIVES	SUGGESTED ACTIVITIES	RESOURCE MATERIAL
A> Muhammad (S), the last Prophet of Allah	**The Children will:** -know that Muhammad (S) was the final prophet, and there will be no prophets after him. -know that if anyone claims to be the prophet after Muhammad (S), he/she is lying.	**The Teacher will:** a. Remind the children about the life of Muhammad (S), relating it with lessons from the Sirah and Islamic History. b. Help the children understand that Allah has told us there will be no more messengers after the Prophet Muhammad (S) in the Qur'an. c. Ask the children what they would say or think if someone claimed to be a prophet. How would they know he/she was lying? (By reading the Qur'an)	

Unit 6:   The Duties of a Muslim: Salah

lesson 1-3

UNIT SIX

LEARNING EXPERIENCES AND ACTIVITIES

1. Learning Concepts (Moral Perspective)

Obligations of a Muslim, concept of 'obligation"
Salah, the obligatory prayer
Meaning of *Salah*
Number of times Muslims should pray
Adab of *Salah*

2. Learning Skills and Attitudes

Vocabulary
Regularity
Steps of *Salah*
Adab of Salah
Memorization of *Suwar*
Cleanliness
Punctuality
Following the *Imam* during *Salah*

3. Artistic Perspective

Rhythm
Coloring, pasting and drawing

TIME REQUIREMENTS

Time Needed: Three class periods (45 minutes each)

10 to 15 minutes each day of the class for
the memorization of the *Suwar*

IQRA' KINDERGARTEN CURRICULUM
FIQH AND IBADAT
UNIT 6: THE DUTIES OF A MUSLIM - SALAH
Lesson 1: Muslims Must Pray Five Times a Day

FOCAL POINT	PERFORMANCE OBJECTIVES	SUGGESTED ACTIVITIES	RESOURCE MATERIAL

A> *Salah* is the duty of every Muslim	**The Children will:**
	
	-learn what Salah is, and that it is compulsory on all Muslims.
	
	-learn that when possible they should offer Salah in congregation.
		The Teacher will:
		
		a. Introduce the lesson by showing the children pictures of people praying or of *Masajid*, and solicit discussion leading to the act of praying.
		
		b. Ask related questions:
		   -*Why do we pray?*
		   -*How many times a day do we pray?*
		   -*What are the names of the different prayers?* etc.
			Pictures of *Masajid* and People praying

B> Prayer is above all other activities	-learn that we must pray regardless of what we are doing, even when travelling. -know that when the time for Salah has arrived, Muslims should stop what they are doing, and pray.	a. Discuss the timings (not exactly) of the daily prayers, b. Show the children pictures of people praying in a *Masjid*, at home, in the garden, on a ship etc., to convey the message that no matter where we are, we should pray when the time of prayer arrives. (See A̲) c. If not already implemented, make a plan where all the classes in the school pray the Salah together at the same time. Make sure, that the plan is such that no class is ever late for Salah. d. Discuss with the principal the possibility of having a student call the *Adhan* on the intercom every day during the prayer time. If this is not possible have one of the children in the class call the *Adhan*.	Worksheet, Crayons, Markers, etc.

PRAY SALAH WHEREVER YOU ARE

IN THE *MASJID*

AT HOME

IN THE SCHOOL

PRAY SALAH WHEREVER YOU ARE

In the Garden

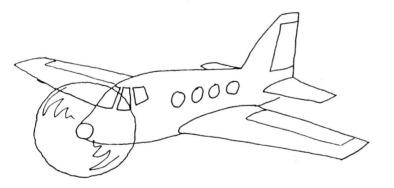

In the Plane

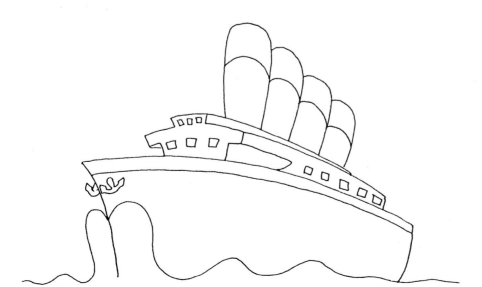

On the Ship

65

IQRA' KINDERGARTEN CURRICULUM
FIQH AND IBADAT
UNIT 6: THE DUTIES OF A MUSLIM - SALAH
Lesson 2: The *Adab* of Salah

FOCAL POINT	PERFORMANCE OBJECTIVES	SUGGESTED ACTIVITIES	RESOURCE MATERIAL
A> Behavior during *Salah*.	The Children will: -develop a habit of being quiet and respectful during *Jama't*. -learn that they must form a straight line, standing shoulder to shoulder, while praying, and not fidget or push each other.	**The Teacher will:** **a.** Talk to the children about the *Adab* of praying Salah. Emphasize the obligation of standing shoulder to shoulder, and being quiet, without talking. **b.** Tell the children that prayer is like standing directly in front of Allah (SWT), and therefore, they should stand with attention and respect. Let them know that prayer is direct communication between them and Allah (SWT).	
B> Keep eyes low while praying	-learn to keep their eyes low, on the ground while praying rather than looking around.	**a.** Stand in line with the children helping them to keep their eyes low, and not looking around. **b.** Deal firmly with those children who push others and create trouble during Salah. **c.** Make sure that the children follow the Imam properly. **d.** Give the children the worksheet of *Adab* of Salah to color and talk about.. (See A)	Worksheets, Crayons

THE ADAB OF SALAH

Below are paired pictures of people praying in different ways. Pick which is right. Then cross out the wrong picture, and color the right one.

| FOLLOWING THE IMAM | PLAYING AROUND |
| HEJAB | NO HEJAB |

IQRA' KINDERGARTEN CURRICULUM
FIQH AND IBADAT
UNIT 6: THE DUTIES OF A MUSLIM - SALAH
Lesson 2: The Adab of Salah
Worksheet A

THE ADAB OF SALAH

Below are paired pictures of people praying in different ways. Pick which is right. Then cross out the wrong picture, and color the right one.

TALK TO YOUR FRIENDS

KEEP QUIET

STAND IN A STRAIGHT LINE

STAND IN A CROOKED LINE

THE ADAB OF SALAH

Below are paired pictures of people praying in different ways. Pick which is right. Then cross out the wrong picture, and color the right one.

| LOOK AROUND | LOOK DOWN |
| STAND STILL | PUSH EACH OTHER |

IQRA' KINDERGARTEN CURRICULUM
FIQH AND IBADAT
UNIT 6: THE DUTIES OF A MUSLIM - SALAH
Lesson 3: *Surahs and Dua's Recited During Salah*

FOCAL POINT	PERFORMANCE OBJECTIVES	SUGGESTED ACTIVITIES	RESOURCE MATERIAL
A> Memorization of *Surahs and Dua'* during Salah	**The Children will:** -begin to memorize and learn all the necessary *Dua's and Surahs* recited during *Salah*.	**The Teacher will:** **a.** Help the children memorize Surat ul-Fatiha and learn to say it during *Qiyam*. Make sure that all the children have learned and can recite the Surah*. **b.** Help the children learn to say the *Takbir*, and know its proper place in prayer. **c.** Help the children learn other short *Surahs* to recite during *Salah*, after *Surat ul-Fatiha*. **d.** Practice *Salah* with the children in class everyday, before going to the prayer hall to pray in congregation.	

* The children may already have learned *Surat ul-Fatiha* and other short *Surahs* during *Qur'anic Studies*, or at home. If this is the case, just review the *Surahs* with them. Help those who may be behind in learning these *Surahs*.

IQRA KINDERGARTEN CURRICULUM
Fiqh and Ibadat
Unit 6: Duties of a Muslim Salah
Lesson 3: Surahs and Dua's recited during salah
Worksheet A: Surat ul-Fatiha Flannel Board Activity

SURAT UL-FATIHA FLANNEL BOARD ACTIVITY

Objectives:

1. Develop a visual conception of the verses of Surat ul-Fatiha

2. Coordinating visual and audio appreciation of the Surah.

Needed Materials:

- one flannel board
- felt
- construction paper
- markers
- clear glue
- scissors
- copy of Surat ul-Fatiha with large script (use xerox machine to enlarge size)

Directions:

1. Cut each Ayah in large strips.

2. Paste each strip on to the same size strips of felt.

3. Always remember to have *Bismillah ir-Rahman ir-Rahim* to be put on top
   of each Surah.

4. Use each strip on the flannel board, as you go along reading and working with the children..

Unit 7: The Duties of a Muslim- Saum

lessons 1-4

UNIT SEVEN

LEARNING EXPERIENCES AND ACTIVITIES

1. Learning Concepts (Moral Perspective)

Meaning and concept of *Saum*
What does it involve to fast?
Concept of fasting to please only Allah (SWT)
Ramadan, the month of fasting
The duration of fast each day
Good deeds during Ramadan
What can young children do to please Allah (SWT) during Ramadan
Concept of following the *Sunnah* of Prophet Muhammad (S)

2. Learning Skills and Attitudes

Vocabulary
listening
Oral language
Sharing
patience
Compassion
Punctuality
Critical thinking

3. Artistic Perspective

Coloring and pasting
Drama and acting
Singing and finger play

TIME REQUIREMENTS

Time Needed: Three class hours (45 minutes each)
One class hours for the evaluation of Units 6 & 7

IQRA' KINDERGARTEN CURRICULUM
FIQH AND IBADAT
UNIT 7: THE DUTIES OF A MUSLIM - FASTING
Lesson 1: The Essence of *Sawm*

FOCAL POINT	PERFORMANCE OBJECTIVES	SUGGESTED ACTIVITIES	RESOURCE MATERIAL
A> Meaning of Sawm (Fasting)	**The Children will:** -develop a concept of *Sawm* and what it involves.	**The Teacher will:** **a.** Introduce the concept of fasting to children closer to the month of Ramadan. Tell the children that fasting is not eating or drinking anything for a period of time (all day long in our case).	
B> The month of fasting	-know that every Muslim must fast during the month of Ramadan (after a certain age). -learn that the month of fasting is called Ramadan. -learn that Ramadan is an Islamic month.	**a.** Tell the children that Allah (SWT) has asked Muslims to fast in the month of Ramadan. **b.** Solicit from the children their own family experiences during Ramadan, and write language experience stories about Ramadan. **c.** Develop an understanding of the Islamic calendar, and count down the days to the moon sighting in Ramadan. **d.** When Ramadan is near sing "Welcome Ramadan" songs. **e.** Try to arrange a Ramadan *Iftar* (fast-breaking) party, where all the parents of the children bring in food, and everyone eats and prays *Maghrib* together. **f.** If possible arrange a class field trip to the local Masjid for *Iftar*. **g.** Have the children do the coloring activity on the Iftar party. (See A)	Worksheet, Crayons

IFTAR PARTY!

Fatimah has invited her friends over for an *Iftar* party on the first day of Ramadan. There's a lot of food - do you know what all of it is? Color the food in quickly - it's almost time for them to break their fast!

76

IQRA' KINDERGARTEN CURRICULUM
FIQH AND IBADAT
UNIT 7: THE DUTIES OF A MUSLIM - FASTING
Lesson 2: The Duration of Sawm

FOCAL POINT	PERFORMANCE OBJECTIVES	SUGGESTED ACTIVITIES	RESOURCE MATERIAL
A> The Duration of Sawm	**The Children will:** -learn that fasting begins at dawn, and ends at sunset.	**The Teacher will:** a. Tell the children that fasting lasts from sunrise to sunset (*Fajr* to *Maghrib*). b. Discuss with the children the meaning of the words *Sahur* and *Iftar*. Then ask if any of the children get up early to eat *Sahur* with the elders in the family. c. Have a discussion with the children about what they eat and do during *Sahur* and *Iftar* in their houses, and write language experience stories. d. Work with the children to prepare a bulletin board of "My Favorite Foods for *Iftar*", on which they paste or draw pictures of their favorite foods.	Scissors, Markers, Pictures of food items, Glue, etc.
B> The *Sunnah* of the Prophet (S) during *Iftar*	-know and follow the *Sunnah* of Muhammad (S) while opening the fast	a. Discuss with the children the favorite foods of the Prophet (S), and tell them that we should start the *Iftar* with dates, as he did. Have the children do the worksheet on the Prophet's (S) favorite foods. (See A)	Worksheets, Crayons

PROPHET MUHAMMAD'S (S) FAVORITE FOODS

Here are some of the favorite foods of Prophet Muhammad (S). How well can you color the food?

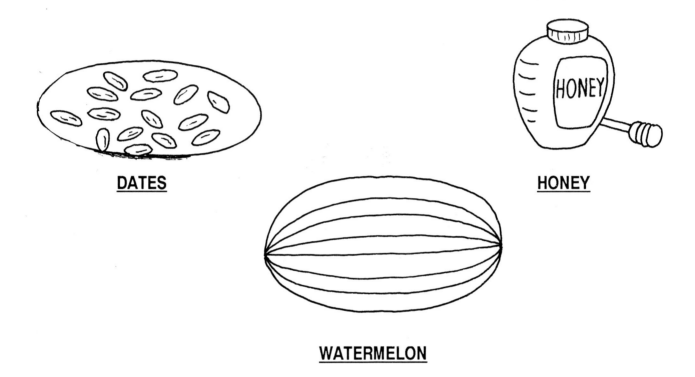

DATES

HONEY

WATERMELON

BREAD

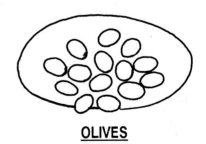

OLIVES

IQRA' KINDERGARTEN CURRICULUM
FIQH AND IBADAT
UNIT 7: THE DUTIES OF A MUSLIM - FASTING
Lesson 3: Doing Good Deeds in Ramadan

FOCAL POINT	PERFORMANCE OBJECTIVES	SUGGESTED ACTIVITIES	RESOURCE MATERIAL
A> Acts of worship during Ramadan	**The Children will:** -understand that Ramadan entails doing good deeds, such as praying, reading Qur'an, not fighting or using bad words with other people, etc. -learn to share their food during Iftar. -learn that we exchange gifts for Eid, and give money and food to the needy.	**The Teacher will:** a. Tell the children that Allah (SWT) has promised to give extra reward to those people who do good deeds during Ramadan. b. Have the children do the coloring exercise on good deeds. After they are done coloring the worksheet, have them cut out the pictures to make flashcards (See <u>A</u>) c. Ask the children what good deeds they have ever done and write language experience stories. d. Have the children make Eid cards and gifts for each other. e. Organize a canned food drive for the hungry. Coordinate this food drive with other classes and grades.	Worksheets, Crayons, Markers, etc.

MY GOOD DEEDS

Color in the pictures of the people doing good deeds. When you are done, cut out the pictures to make yourself a set of flashcards.

USE GOOD LANGUAGE

VISIT THE SICK

HELP OTHERS

AVOID FIGHTS

KEEP CLEAN

READ QUR'AN

SHARE FOOD WITH OTHERS

PRAY SALAH

CLEAN UP AROUND YOU

STUDY HARD

IQRA' KINDERGARTEN CURRICULUM
FIQH AND IBADAT
UNIT 7: THE DUTIES OF A MUSLIM - FASTING
Lesson 4: The Celebration of Eid `

FOCAL POINT	PERFORMANCE OBJECTIVES	SUGGESTED ACTIVITIES	RESOURCE MATERIAL
A> The meaning of Eid	The Children will: -count the days on the calendar to the sighting of the moon for Eid. -learn that Eid is the celebration of the end of fasting. -learn that all Muslims go to communal Eid prayer to thank Allah (SWT) for helping them fast and obey Him. -know that on Eid day we cannot fast.	The Teacher will: a. Start counting the days to Eid on the Ramadan calendar. b. Tell the children that we pray the Eid Salah to thank Allah (SWT) for helping us to fast and obey Him during the month of Ramadan. c. Work with the children to prepare and mail Eid cards to their friends and parents. d. Plan to have an Eid party in the classroom.	Construction Paper, Scissors, Glue, etc.

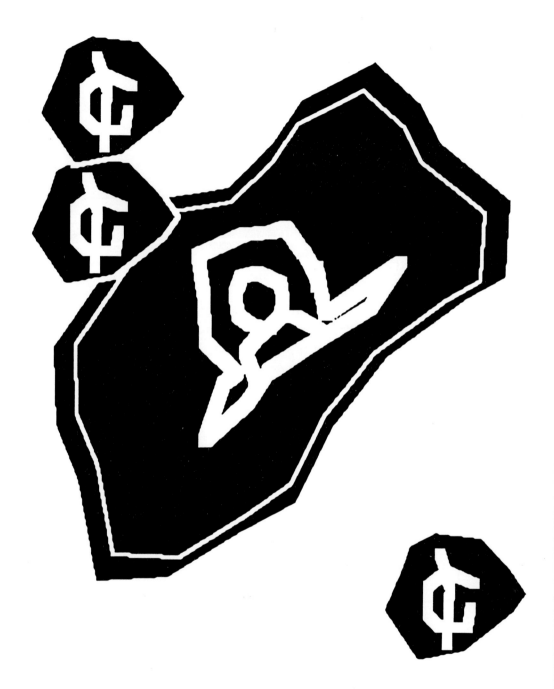

Unit 8: The Duties of a Muslim: Zakat

lesson 1

UNIT EIGHT

LEARNING EXPERIENCES AND ACTIVITIES

1. Learning Concepts (Moral Perspective)

Obedience to Allah's Commands
Concept of sharing
Sharing with those who have less
Sharing with family and friends
Every thing we have comes from Allah (SWT)

2. Learning Skills and Attitudes

Vocabulary
Oral language
Willingness to share
Joys of sharing
Working to help the poor and the needy

3. Artistic Perspective

Singing
Coloring

TIME REQUIREMENTS

Time Needed: Two class hours (45 minutes each)

IQRA' KINDERGARTEN CURRICULUM
FIQH AND IBADAT
UNIT 8: THE DUTIES OF A MUSLIM - ZAKAT
Lesson 1: Sharing with the Needy

FOCAL POINT	PERFORMANCE OBJECTIVES	SUGGESTED ACTIVITIES	RESOURCE MATERIAL
A> The concept of sharing	**The Children will:** -learn the virtue of sharing with others. -learn to give to the needy. -learn that they can share a lot more then just money -learn to share their toys with each other.	**The Teacher will:** **a.** Discuss the concept of sharing whatever Allah (SWT) has given us, as everything belongs to Him anyway. **b.** Try to expand the children's concept of sharing, by telling them that money is not the only gift of Allah (SWT) that we share. We also share our clothes, time, knowledge, and any talent or skill given to us by Allah (SWT). **c.** Explain to the children that there are millions of people and children across the world who have no place to live or sleep and nothing to eat or drink, and nothing to wear. Show them pictures or videos of homeless people and poorer nations so they gain an understanding. **d.** Organize a canned food or clothes drive or activities which will act as a relief effort whilst allowing the children to share their possessions with the less fortunate.	Pictures or Video Tapes

Unit 9:   The Duties of a Muslim: Hajj

lesson 1-2

UNIT NINE

Learning Experiences and Activities

1. Learning Concepts (Moral Perspectives)

Meaning of *Hajj*
Concept of *Hajj*
Meaning and concept of Obligatory
Requirement of a specific time of the year to perform *Hajj - Dul Hijjah*
Hajji, the person who performs *Hajj*
Respect for a *Hajji*
Concept of the Muslim *Ummah* from around the world

2. Learning Skills and Attitudes

Vocabulary
Location and direction of the Kabah
Means of transportation
Calculation of the time it would take to fly to Jeddah -- from New York, London etc.
Duration of *Hajj*
Critical thinking skills

3. Artistic Perspective

Dressing up/ role playing
singing/ recitation
cutting, pasting and coloring

TIME REQUIREMENTS

Time Needed: Three Class hours (45 minutes each)

IQRA' KINDERGARTEN CURRICULUM
FIQH AND IBADAT
UNIT 9: THE DUTIES OF A MUSLIM - *HAJJ*
Lesson 1: *Hajj* is Required of all Muslims

FOCAL POINT	PERFORMANCE OBJECTIVES	SUGGESTED ACTIVITIES	RESOURCE MATERIAL
A> *Hajj* is an obligation	**The Children will:** -know that as Muslims we should do everything to please Allah (SWT). -learn that *Hajj* is compulsory for all Muslims who can afford it. -learn that people can only do *Hajj* during a certain part of the year.	**The Teacher will:** a. Tell the children that there are many things we can do to please Allah (SWT), such as praying, fasting, giving Zakat, helping other people, etc. Tell them that another action that pleases Allah (SWT) is when a Muslim does *Hajj*, and visits the House of Allah (*Kabah*). Help the children recall the lesson about Prophet Ibrahim building the Kabah, from Islamic History. b. Tell the children that people can only perform *Hajj* in the month of *Dhul-Hijjah*. Show the children an Islamic calendar, and point out the month of *Hajj*.	The Story of Ibrahim (A) Iqra' Int.. Educational Foundation. Islamic Calendar

IQRA' KINDERGARTEN CURRICULUM
FIQH AND IBADAT
UNIT 9: THE DUTIES OF A MUSLIM - *HAJJ*
Lesson 2: The Requirements of a *Hajji*

FOCAL POINT	PERFORMANCE OBJECTIVES	SUGGESTED ACTIVITIES	RESOURCE MATERIAL
A> The term *Hajji*	**The Children will:** -learn that a person who does *Hajj* is called a *Hajji or Hajjah*. -know that a *Hajji* must wear an *Ehram*.	**The Teacher will:** **a.** Share pictures or slides of people in *Hajj*, wearing *Ehrams*, and tell the children that these people are called *Hajji or Hajjah*. Show the children how everyone looks the same and there is no differentiation, so nobody is better than anyone else. **b.** Tell the children the *Ehram* requirements for both males and females. Bring in child size *Ehram* garments, and try them on the boys and girls. **c.** Let the children know that the people must keep the *Ehram* on until the *Hajj* is over.	Pictures or Movies of people in *Hajj* *Ehram* for boys and girls
B> Respect for a *Hajji or Hajjah*	-learn that they must show respect to any people who have completed *Hajj*.	**a.** Tell the children that as Muslims we should respect any *Hajji or Hajjah*. **b.** Invite a *Hajji or Hajjah* to the class to talk about his/her experiences during *Hajj*. **c.** Tell the children that every *Hajji/Hajjah* must do certain things in *Hajj*: -walk around the *Kabah* seven times between the hills of *Saffa and Marwa* seven times must not get angry or kill any living being must keep clean must remember Allah a lot and read Qur'an, etc. **d.** Conclude the lesson with a comprehension exercise.	

Unit 10: The Forbidden and Permitted in Islam

lessons 1-3

UNIT TEN

LEARNING EXPERIENCES AND ACTIVITIES

1. Learning Concepts (Moral Perspectives)

Concept of *Halal & Haram*
Responsibility of a Muslim to adopt *Halal* practices
Serving the parents (love, care obedience)
Concept of *Halal & haram* in foods and drinks
Concept of Islamic dress codes
Need to follow the dress code
Concept of pleasing Allah (SWT) through our actions and thoughts

2. Learning Skills and Attitudes

Vocabulary
Positive and respectful attitude towards the parents
Willingness to please and serve the parents
Using the Islamic greetings
Addressing adults with respect and honor
Using proper language
Following Islamic dietary regulations
Willingness to share the dietary code with friends and teachers at school with the friends and the teachers
Following Islamic dress code

3. Artistic Expressions

Singing
Dramatic play
Coloring and pasting

TIME REQUIREMENTS

Time Needed: Three class hours (45 minutes each)
Two class hours for the revision and evaluation of
entire KG curriculum of Fiqh and 'Ibadat.

96

IQRA' KINDERGARTEN CURRICULUM
FIQH AND IBADAT
UNIT 10: THE FORBIDDEN AND PERMITTED IN ISLAM
Lesson 1: Respect for Parents and Elders

FOCAL POINT	PERFORMANCE OBJECTIVES	SUGGESTED ACTIVITIES	RESOURCE MATERIAL
A> Respect for parents and elders	The Children will: -learn to respect their parents, teachers and other elders. -greet adults and parents with *Assalamu Alaikum*, and address them as Mr., Mrs., Brother, Sister, Uncle, or Aunt_____ etc. -learn that they should never disobey or disrespect their parents and elders.	The Teacher will: a. Help children remember the *Hadith* in which we are asked to help our parents. b. Ask the children why they think Allah (SWT) and the Prophet (S) have told us to respect and obey our parents. Use the children's answers as language experience stories. c. Make sure that the children call every teacher and other elders in the school with some honorable title, like "Brother Mahmoud", "Sister Fatimah", etc. Tell them that when they meet a Muslim they should greet them with *Assalamu Alaikum*. d. Tell the children that when an adult talks to them they should listen to them attentively and show them respect. e. Have a special discussion with the class on the importance of obedience to parents.	

IQRA' KINDERGARTEN CURRICULUM
FIQH AND IBADAT
UNIT 10: THE FORBIDDEN AND PERMITTED IN ISLAM
Lesson 2: Eating and Drinking

FOCAL POINT	PERFORMANCE OBJECTIVES	SUGGESTED ACTIVITIES	RESOURCE MATERIAL
A> *Halal and Haram* foods and drinks	**The Children will:** -learn that Allah (SWT) has permitted us to eat many kinds of food, but has forbidden us to eat certain types. -learn the types of food and drink Allah (SWT) has forbidden us to eat.	**The Teacher will:** **a.** Talk about foods that are healthy for us and foods that are bad for us, etc. Tell the children that Allah (SWT) knows best and he has forbidden us from eating certain foods. **b.** Share pictures of foods we cannot eat with the children, For example; -meat that comes from the pig (or products made form the pig) -meat from animals slaughtered without saying Allah's name -birds of prey (meat eating birds) -beverages which contain alcohol	Pictures of food and drinks that are Haram in Islam

IQRA' KINDERGARTEN CURRICULUM
FIQH AND IBADAT
UNIT 10: THE FORBIDDENT AND THE PERMITTED IN ISLAM
Leson 2: Eating and Drinking

Color the pictures of the animals and the birds below.
Cross Out (X) out the ones whose meat is *Haram*.

IQRA' KINDERGARTEN CURRICULUM
FIQH AND IBADAT
UNIT 10: THE FORBIDDEN AND PERMITTED IN ISLAM
Lesson 3: The Islamic Dress Code

FOCAL POINT	PERFORMANCE OBJECTIVES	SUGGESTED ACTIVITIES	RESOURCE MATERIAL
A> *Satar* for men and women	**The Children will:** -learn the meaning of the word *Satar* at their own level. -learn that Muslims dress modestly and wear clean clothes.	**The Teacher will:** a. Share illustrations or pictures of people dressed in proper satar, (women in scarves and long dresses, and men with proper attire.) b. Discuss with the children that females are expected to cover most parts of their bodies after a certain age and men are required to dress modestly. c. Tell the children that we should wear clothes that are modest and unrevealing. Tell the children that they should be careful to wash their hands after painting or eating or playing, etc.	Pictures, Slides, etc of people in Satar

Circle the pictures which show how a Muslim should dress.

Kindergarten Curriculum Evaluation Form.

subject: _____ unit: _____ lesson: _____

PHILOSOPHY	STRONGLY AGREE	AGREE	NO OPINION	DISAGREE
The philosophy of the program is sound.				
The philosophy needs clarification.				
DESIGN (curriculum organization)	STRONGLY AGREE	AGREE	NO OPINION	DISAGREE
The design is well arranged.				
The following components are well defined and arranged:				
i) aims and objectives				
ii) subject matter				
iii) activities				
iv) needed materials				
SCOPE & SEQUENCE	STRONGLY AGREE	AGREE	NO OPINION	DISAGREE
Covers enough subject matter at this level.				
Selection of objectives, subject matter and activities is well sequenced (proceeds from easy to difficult.)				
TIME FRAME	STRONGLY AGREE	AGREE	NO OPINION	DISAGREE
Enough time is provided for each lesson.				
This lesson needs more time.				
This lesson needs less time.				

We would appreciate it if you would photocopy this form and evaluate each lesson.
Please mail to: **Curriculum Evaluation Response**
IQRA' International Educational Foundation
831 South Laflin
Chicago, Il 60607

102

Comments...
Please support your evaluation by summarizing your comments below:

_____

_____

_____

_____

_____

_____

_____

_____

_____

_____

_____

_____

_____

_____

_____

_____

_____

_____

name _____

street _____

city _____ state _____ zip code _____

phone number ( ) - _____ - _____   103

position affiliation _____

بِسْمِ ٱللّٰهِ ٱلرَّحْمٰنِ ٱلرَّحِيمِ

IQRA' KINDERGARTEN CURRICULUM FIQH AND 'IBADAT

REFERENCES FOR TEACHERS

Arabic:

فقه السنّة لسَيّد سابق

English:

Fiqh-us- Sunnah by Sayyid Sabiq
American Trust Publication

Urdu:

آسان فقه - حصة اولی - مولانا اصلاحي

آسان فقه - حصة ثانية

These books are available at IQRA' BOOK CENTER
6410 N. Campbell Ave.
Chicago, Il 60645
(312) 274-2665

Barron, L.   Mathematics Experiences for the Early Childhood Years. Columbus, Ohio:
                                    Charles E. Merril Publishing Co., 1979.

Charlesworth, R.,   Experiences in Math for Young Children. Albany, N.Y.:
and Radeloff, D.   Delmar Publishers, 1978.

DeVires, Rheta and   Constructive Early Education: Overview and Comparison with Other
Kohlberg, Lawrence.   Programs. Washington D.C.: Association for the Education of Young
Children, 1990.

Harns, Christine A.   Child Development. West Publishing Company, 1986.

Harlan, J.D.   Science Experiences for the Early Childhood Years, 2nd ed. Columbus,
                                    Ohio: Charles E. Merril Publishing Co., 1980.

Hickman, Jane and   Children's Literature in the Classroom. Christopher Gordon
Cullinan, Bernice, ed.   Publishing Co., 1989.

Hill, K.   Exploring the Natural World with Young Children.
                                    Harcourt, Brace, Jovanovich, 1976.

Kamii, C. and   Piaget Children and Humben. Washington D.C.: National Association for the
DeVries, R.   Education of Young Children, 1984.

Machado, Jeanne M.   Early Childhood Experiences in Language Arts.
                                    Delmar Publishing Co., 1985.

Mayesky, Mary, and   Creative Activities for Young Children. Delmar Publishing Co., 1985.
Herman, Donald, and
Wlodkowski.

National Geographic   Books for Young Explorers Series. Washington D.C.: National
Society.   Geographic Society, 1974.

Payne, J.H. Ed.   Mathematics Learning in Early Childhood. Reston, VA:
                                    The National Council of Mathematics, 1975.

Scott, L.B. and   Mathematical Experiences for Kindergarten and Primary Teachers.
Garner, J.   New York: McGraw Hill, 1978.

FAVORITE BOOKS FOR KINDERGARTNERS

Alborough, Jez.   <u>Esther's Trunk</u>. Warner, 1989.

Bemelmans, Ludwig.   <u>Madeline</u>. Viking Press, 1939.

Bemelmans, Ludwig.   <u>Madeline's Rescue</u>.

Bennett, David.   <u>One Cow Moo Moo</u>. Holt, 1991.

Bozzo, Maxine.   <u>Toby in the Country, Toby in the City</u>. Greenwillow, 1982.

Brown, Marcia.   <u>The Three Little Billy Goats Gruff</u>.

Brown, Margaret Z.   <u>Goodnight Moon</u>. Harper, 1947.

Brunhoff, Laurent de.   <u>Babar's Little Circus Star</u>. Random House, 1989.

Burton, Virginia L.   <u>The Little House</u>. Houghton Mifflin, 1942.

Burton, Virginia L.   <u>Mike Mulligan and His Steam Shovel</u>. Houghton Mifflin, 1939.

Calhoun, Mary.   <u>Cross-country Cat</u>. Morrow, 1979.

Christelow, Eileen.   <u>Five Little Monkeys Jumping on the Bed</u>. Clarion Press, 1990.

Cherry, Lynne.   <u>Who's Sick Today</u>? Dutton, 1989.

Cliff, Patricia Rilly.   <u>Ronald Morgan Goes to Bat</u>. Viking Press, 1989.

Clifton, Lucille.   <u>My Friend Jacob</u>. Dutton, 1980.

Cohen, Miriam.   <u>Will I Have a Friend</u>? Macmillan, 1967.

Cole, Joanna.   <u>It's Too Noisy</u>! Crowell, 1990.

Conrad, Pam.   <u>The Tub People</u>. Harper, Collins, 1990.

Crews, Donald.   <u>Freight Train</u>. Greenwillow, 1978.

Crews, Donald.   <u>Light</u>. Greenwillow

Daugherty, James H.   <u>Andy and the Lion</u>. Viking Press, 1938.

Davis, Jim.   <u>Garfield's Furry Tales</u>. Grosset, 1990.

Delton, Judy.   <u>My Mom Made Me Go To Camp</u>. Delacorte, 1991.

De Paola, Tomie.   <u>Charlie Needs a Clock</u>. Prentice Hall, 1973.

Dinardo, Jeffery.   <u>The Wolf Who Cried Boy</u>. Grosset, 1990.

Ehlert, Lois.   <u>Fish Eyes: A Book You Can Count On</u>. H.B.J., 1991.

Eyles, Heather.   <u>A Zoo in Our House</u>. Warner, 1989.

Flack, Marjorie.   <u>Ask Mr. Bear</u>. Macmillan, 1932.

Freeman, Don.   <u>Corduroy</u>. Viking Press, 1967.

Goig, Wanda.   <u>Millions of Cats</u>. Coward, 1928.

Ginsburg, Mirna.   <u>Across the Stream</u>. Greenwillow, 1982.

Ginsburg, Mirna.   <u>Good Morning, Chick</u>. Greenwillow, 1980.

Goldone, Paul.   <u>The Little Red Hen</u>. Clarion, 1973.

Greene, Carol.   <u>Miss Apple's Hats</u>. Milliken, 1990.

Grossman, Bill.   <u>The Guy Who Was Five Minutes Late</u>. Harper Collins, 1991.

Hoban, Russell.   <u>Bedtime for Frances</u>. Harper, 1960.

Hoban, Russell.   <u>Bread and Jam for Frances</u>.

Hoban, Russell.   <u>A Babysitter for Frances</u>.

Hoban, Russell.   <u>A Birthday for Frances</u>.

Hogrogian, Nonny.   <u>One Fine Day</u>. Macmillan, 1971.

Hurd, Edith T.   <u>I Dance in My Red Pajamas</u>. Harper, 1982.

Kents, Ezra J.   <u>The Snowy Day</u>. Viking Press, 1962.

Kraus, Robert.   <u>The Mixed-up Mice Clean House</u>. Warner, 1991.

Lionni, Leo.   <u>Frederick</u>. Pantheon, 1966.

Lobel, Arnold.   <u>On Market Street</u>. Greenwillow, 1981.

McCloskey, Robert.   <u>Make Way for Ducklings</u>. Viking Press, 1941.

McPhail, David.   <u>Lost</u>! Joystreet, 1991.

Marshall, James.   <u>George and Martha</u>. Houghton, 1972.

Nerlove, Miriam.   <u>Just One Tooth</u>. McElderry, 1990

Oppenheim, Joanne.   "<u>Not Now</u>!" Said the Cow. Bantam, 1990.

Paresh, Peggy.   <u>Good Hunting, Blue Sky</u>. Harper, Collins, 1989.

Paris, Pat.   <u>The Frog</u>. Simon & Schuster, 1990.

Polette, Keith.   The Winter Duckling. Milliken, 1991.

Potter, Beatrix.   Where's Peter Rabbit? Viking Press, 1989.

Rey, Hans A.   Curious George. Houghton, 1941.

Ross, Tony.   Oscar Got the Blame.

Sendak, Maurice.   Where the Wild Things Are. Harper, 1963.

Seuss, Dr.   The Cat in the Hat. Random House, 1957.

Slobodkina, Esphyr.   Caps for Sale. Addison, 1947.

Spier, Peter.   Noah's Ark. Doubleday, 1977. -

Steig, William.   Sylvester and the Magic Pebble. Windmill, 1969.

Stock, Catherine.   A Little Elephant's ABC. Clarion Press, 1989.

Thacher, Hund.   Blackberry Rumble. Crown Books, 1991.

Thompson, Carol.   Time. Delacorte

Wells, Rosemary.   Timothy Goes to School. Dial, 1981.

Wah, Jan.   The Adventures of Underwater Dog. Grosset, 1990.

Walsh, Ellen S.   Mouse Paint. Harcourt, Brace, Jovanovich, 1990.

Zelinsky, Paul.   The Maid and the Mouse and the Odd-shaped House. Dodd, 1981.

Zion, Gene.   Harry, the Dirty Dog. Harper, 1956.

Zion, Gene.   No Roses for Harry. Harper, 1956.

Zion, Gene.   Harry By the Sea. Harper, 1956.

Rockwell, Anne.   The Three Bears and Fifteen Other Stories. Crowell, 1975.

Thomas, Patricia.   "Stand Back" said the Elephant, "I'm Going to Sneeze!", Lothrop, 1991.

IQRA' Islamic History Kindergarten Curriculum

Scope and Sequence

GRADE LEVELS

K-6

Aqidah and Fiqh
Islamic Manners

Scope and Sequence: *Aqidah and Fiqh*

K	1	2	3
Identity Islamic Greetings Oneness of Allah The Prophets Angels Books of Allah Salah--Adab of Salah sharing	Arakan Shahadah Tawid Risalah Mala'ikah Al'-Akhirah	Salah Saum 'id-ul-fitr Zakah Earning a living Hajj	The Believer Islamic brotherhood Ummah Shahadah Angels Prophets Scriptures Akhirah Qiyamah The Qadr (detailed study of above topics)

4	5	6

SALAH
Meaning
Names
Timings
Ways to Pray
Numbers of Rakhas
Requirements for Salah
  Wudu
  Taymum
  Adhan
Contents of Salah
  Niyyah
  Takbir
  Qiyam
  Ruku
  Sujud
  Jalasah etc.
	SAUM
	Qur'anic Verses & Ahadith
	  enjoining Saum
	Ramadan
	Sighting of the moon
	Importance
	Barakah
	Lailatul Qadr
	Duration
	Suhur & Iftar
	Niyah-Du'a
	Requirements
	Kifayah
	Kinds of Fast
	Taraviah Prayers
	Aeteka
	Sadeqa Fitr.
	
	ZAKAT
	Meaning
	Nisab
	Collection
	Distribution
	Payment in kind
	Bait-ul-mal
	Sharing concept
		HAJJ
		Meaning
		Historical Background
		Importance
		Ayahs & Ahadith
		  enjoining Hajj
		Virtues & Benefits
		Requirements for eligibility
		Steps in performing Hajj
		Ahram, Nafl, Niyah
		Journey to Makkah, *Tawaf,*
		Sai, Stay in *Mena,* Stay
		in *'Arafah, Muzdalfah,*
		Rami, Sacrifice
		Clipping or shaving of hair
		Taking the *Ahram* off,
		Tw'af of Wida'
		Visit to Madinah
		Hajj Badl
		
		JIHAD
		Meaning
		Concept
		Qur'anic injunction
		Ahadith

110

Scope and Sequence: *Islamic Manners*

K

Islamic Greetings
Dua for-
  Eating
  Travel
  Entering a building

Respect for
  Parents
  Teachers
  Elders
  Use of Islamic language
  Proper vocabulary

1

Family Members
  Respect
  Love
  Care

Islamic values
  Cleanliness
  Manners of dress
  Mannerism during meal
  Mannerism during travel
  Relationships with neighbors-
  Muslim and others
  Relationship with other Creations
  of Allah

2

Mannerism
  Inthe Mosque
  At house and school
  In the market
  Ettiquettes of Salah
  Relationships with the parents
  Ettiquettes of friendship

Halal and Halam
  Food
  Earnings
  Spendings
  Dress code

3

Ettiquettes of Conversation
  Proper language
  Slow speed
  Lower voice
  Lower gaze
  Listening attentively
  Listening with care
  No interference during a discourse

Relationship with Environment
  Conservation
  Recycling
  Protection of the echosystem
  Sharing resources
  Thankfulness to Allah

4

Ettiquettes of Salah
  Cleanliness
  Quiteness
  Facing the *Qiblah*
  Punctuality
  Regularity
  Concentration
  Dedication
  Feeling of Allah's prescence

5

Ettiquettes of Saum
  Sighting the moon
  Spending more time in *Ibadat*
  Keeping good behavior
  Avoiding anger
  Sharing *Iftar* and *Suhur*
  Being patient and thankful to Allah

Ettiquettes of Zakat
  Only to please Allah
  No interior motive
  Not arrogance
  Zakat-money should be *Halal*
  Payment on time

6

Ettiquettes of *Hajj*
  Intention to please Allah only
  No worldly motives
  Fulfillment of *Fard*
  Worshipping Allah
  Asking for His forgiveness
  Timely performance
  Single mindedness of the purpose
  A woman to accompany her
  Mahram
  Respect for *Ahram*
  Respect for fellow *Hujjaj*
  Time should be spent in prayers
  Care and humility
  Visit to Madniah
  Offering *Salam* to the prophet(s)
  Respect for the Hujjaj

Introduction
of the
Author

Dr. Tasneema K. Ghazi,
M.A. (Alig.), M.Ed. (Allahabad), Acd.Dip.(London),
CAGS (Harvard), Ph.D. (Minnesota)

Dr. Tasneema Ghazi is Director of Curriculum at IQRA' International Educational Foundation. She is a specialist in Child Development and Reading (Curriculum and Instruction). She has studied at the universities of Aligarh, Allahabad, London, Harvard, San Diego, and Minnesota . She has taught in India, England, United States and Saudi Arabia at various levels: kindergarten, elementary, junior and senior high school and the university. Her most recent appointments have been as Community Professor of Reading and Language Arts at Governor State University, Park Forest South, Illinois, and as Instructor of English Language at Women's College King Abdulaziz University, Jeddah, Saudi Arabia.

Ever since her arrival in the U.S.A. in 1968, she has always been involved with the establishment and organization of schools of Islamic Studies in the United States. Working with children and for children is her main interest.

Dr. Tasneema Ghazi and her husband, Dr. Abidullah Ghazi, are co-founders of IQRA' International. They have given up their professional careers and have committed their lives to developing an *integrated curriculum* and producing *a comprehensive system of Islamic Studies.* They have produced the first model program of *Sirah,* which is in use in most Islamic schools and is being translated in major world languages.

Helped by a team of co-workers, their life's goal is to establish IQRA' International Educational Foundation as a foremost Islamic Educational Research Institution of the Western World.

They have five children. Their children provided them with their first educational experimental lab. They are also their co-workers contributing creatively to IQRA's educational endeavors.

Distributors:

IQRA' Book Center
6410 N. Campbell Ave.
Chicago, IL 60645 U.S.A.

Phone: (312) 274-2665
Toll-Free: (800) 521-ICRA
Fax: (312) 274-8733